In All Things Charity

A Pastoral Challenge for the New Millennium

UNITED STATES CATHOLIC CONFERENCE
WASHINGTON, D.C.

The text of *In All Things Charity: A Pastoral Challenge for the New Millennium* was developed by the Ad Hoc Committee for a Pastoral Message on Charity of the National Conference of Catholic Bishops. It was adopted in November 1999 by the full body of bishops at their general meeting. Its publication is authorized by the undersigned.

Monsignor Dennis M. Schnurr
General Secretary, NCCB/USCC

Photographs: Cover, clockwise: Rick Reinhard, Laura Sikes/Catholic Charities USA, Rick Reinhard, Michael Hoyt; p. iv: Cathy Joyce; p. 2: Karen Callaway; p. 4: Rick Reinhard; p. 10: Michael Hoyt; p. 13: Lisa Kessler; p. 18: Michael Hoyt; p. 22: Jim Whitmer; p. 34: Nancy Wiechec/Catholic News Service; pp. 40 and 43: Rick Reinhard.

First Printing, November 1999

ISBN 1-57455-358-5

Contents

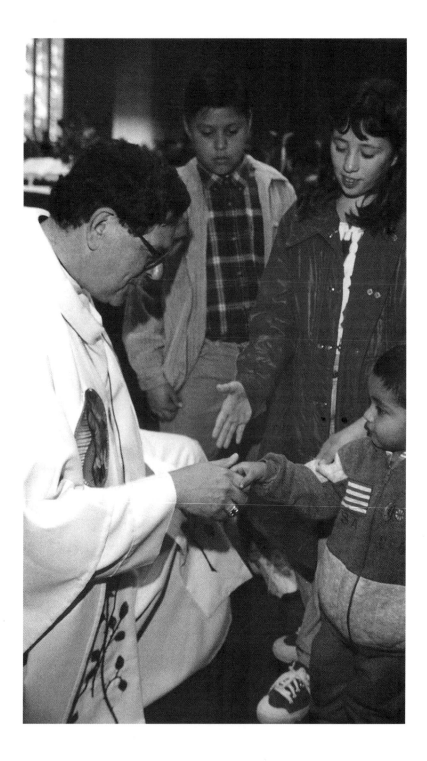

I

Introduction

As we enter a new millennium, the words of Jesus to His disciples ring with renewed significance: "I give you a new commandment: love one another. . . . This is how all will know that you are my disciples, if you have love for one another" (Jn 13:34). With these words, the entire Christian vocation is conveyed in a simple, profound definition of charity. The "new commandment" of charity unites love of God with love of neighbor; it bridges Old and New Testaments; it provides the foundation for human morality; it spans all time and all peoples.

II

A Timely Reflection

ach day we hear about the millions of people who suffer from the agony of hunger and thirst, who have no work or are paid so little that they cannot buy "daily bread" for themselves or their children. We are haunted by images of those who are displaced from their homes and local communities by the ravages of war and violence. In our cities, we confront ever-increasing numbers of people who have no homes or even minimal shelter in which to lay their heads. In our rural areas, we regret the loss of family farms, which have been tilled and passed on from generation to generation and, until recently, have represented the mainstay of our country's food supply. We witness the pain of broken families and the confusion of children who turn to violence as a result of the absence of adult role models at home or school.

We are equally aware of the smiles on faces of refugees and migrants who have been welcomed by parish resettlement committees. Because of the professional counseling services received at Catholic Charities agencies and the love and care received by children adopted through Catholic-sponsored child protection programs, families have found the joy to overcome their pain and division. In addition, the sense of accomplishment among those who have empowered themselves with the assistance of Catholic-sponsored job training programs or through membership in faith-based community organizing efforts has brought joy to many. Those far away from the United States benefit from the assistance and development efforts of Catholic Relief Services and have found hope.

Thus we, the Catholic bishops of the United States, as teachers and pastors express our solidarity with all our brothers and sisters living in poverty or other unjust conditions and to offer thanks and encouragement to those responding to the "cries of those who are poor" through the Church's works of charity, justice, and peace. We write as well to challenge all people of faith and people of good will to greater solidarity with the poor and with those prevented from fulfilling the unique dignity that God has given to all women and men.

THE PLIGHT OF THE WORLD'S POOR

- 43,000 people die of hunger and its consequences every day in all parts of the world, despite the fact that the United States has the global capacity to produce and distribute more than enough food for everyone in the world.
- More than 80 percent of the world's people live in developing countries, but they hold just 20 percent of the world's wealth. The remaining 20 percent live in industrialized nations and hold 80 percent of the world's wealth.
- Of the 4.4 billion people living in developing countries
  — Three-fifths live in communities without basic sanitation.
  — Almost one-third are without safe drinking water.
  — One-quarter lack adequate housing.
  — One-fifth live beyond the reach of modern health services.
  — One-fifth do not proceed beyond a fifth-grade level in school.
  — One-fifth are malnourished.
  — The majority must depend on their feet for transportation to complete daily chores, including the gathering of fuel and water.

Source: United Nations Development Program, *Human Development Report 1998*,
New York: Oxford University Press, 1998

We submit this message at a timely moment in the history of humanity: the threshold of the third millennium, a time when our Holy Father, Pope John Paul II, has called upon us to "open wide the doors to Christ" by making a commitment to justice and peace as an integral condition for the preparation and celebration of the Great Jubilee.[1] This commitment cannot be ignored or excused. The Holy Father states firmly and urgently, "There should be no more postponement of the time when the poor Lazarus can sit beside the rich man to share the same banquet and be forced no more to feed on the scraps that fall from the table (cf. Lk 16:19-31). Extreme poverty is a source of violence, bitterness, and scandal; to eradicate it is the work of justice and therefore of peace."[2] As we set our vision toward the jubilee year and the third millennium, let us pray for the strength and courage to face the pastoral challenge before us: **in all things, charity.**[3]

We must tell the story of human needs

We are shocked and scandalized by the global dimensions of poverty and exclusion. During 1998, while global consumption of goods topped $24 trillion—twice that of 1975—some 4.4 billion people in developing countries had little access to basic goods and services. We are equally concerned that the U.S. government spends less than 1 percent of the federal budget on foreign aid and designates less than one-half of 1 percent to fight world hunger and poverty.[4]

The Special Synodal Assembly for America denounced the "social sins which cry to heaven because they generate violence [and] disrupt peace and harmony between communities within single nations, between nations and between the different regions of the continent."[5] The U.S. bishops and other participants at the synod spoke with grave concern for all persons whose lives are oppressed as a result of these sins, identified as "the drug trade, the recycling of illicit funds, corruption at every level, the terror of

LIVING IN POVERTY IN THE UNITED STATES

- In 1997, 13.3 percent of the U.S. population, or 35,574,000 people, were living below the poverty line (annual income less than $16,400 for a family of four).
- 19.9 percent of our nation's children live in poverty.
- 20 percent of farmers live in poverty.
- 26.5 percent of African Americans and 27.1 percent of Hispanics live in poverty. (These percentages are disproportionate to the representation of these groups in the general U.S. population.)
- Ten years ago, 21.8 million Americans, or 14.8 percent of the population, had no health insurance. Since then, the number without health insurance has increased on average by 1 million annually and now accounts for almost 18 percent of the U.S. population.

Source: U.S. Census Bureau, 1997

violence, the arms race, racial discrimination, inequality between social groups and irrational destruction of nature."[6] They also noted that poverty has an inordinate impact on women and children.

Citizens of the United States find the tragic evidence of poverty and oppression within our own borders. In the midst of an unprecedented "economic boom," far too many of our sisters and brothers live in poverty. Although increased funding has become available for welfare-to-work initiatives and child care programs and many people have been helped to find jobs, low wages leave many families unable to afford rent, groceries, shoes, school supplies, medicine, and bus fare.[7] While the gross national product of the United States grew by almost 25 percent between the years 1980 and 1995, the number of people living in poverty increased by nearly seven million.[8]

In the face of such human suffering, the Church has continued the tradition of its earliest years: to offer physical comfort, healing, emotional support, and spiritual guidance to those who are most beloved by God—the poor and the vulnerable.

Let us celebrate our tradition of service

The history of the Church reveals a long tradition of defending those living in poverty, supporting charitable institutions,[9] and promoting justice. Many religious orders were established on the principles of sharing the goods of the earth with the poor and of recognizing the essential dignity of human persons, without regard to their economic or social status. In most parts of the world, the first hospitals, orphanages, schools, and social service centers were founded by the Church to enlighten the minds of young people and to lift the burden of suffering from those most in need. Faithful to this tradition, the Catholic Church in the United States now sponsors the largest voluntary network of social services, health care, and education in the United States. As a result of the Church's efforts, greater recognition has been given to the inviolability of human life, the sanctity of marriage, the dignity of women, and the value of human work.[10] One of the most effective services to poor children in the United States has been the education provided in Catholic schools.

A celebration of our heritage in charity should be observed with our grateful and joyous acknowledgment of the many holy women and men who shaped our tradition and ministry. Some we know from the pages of Sacred Scripture, and others developed their apostolates centuries later: for example, Sts. Francis and Clare, St. Camillus de Lellis, Sts. Vincent De Paul and Louise de Marillac, Sts. Peter Claver and Martin de Porres, and Blessed Frederick Ozanam. Others enriched the life of the Church in the United States: Sr. Henriette de Lille, St. Elizabeth Ann Seton, St. Frances Xavier Cabrini, Blessed Katharine Drexel, Blessed Padre Junipero Serra, Venerable Pierre Touissant, and Blessed Damien of Moloka'i. We remember the voices of others, such as Msgr. John Ryan, Msgr. John O'Grady, Dorothy Day, Cesar Chavez, Sr. Thea Bowman, and Mother Teresa of Calcutta, who challenged us to deepen our identification with and commitment to people living in poverty.

III

The Message of Scripture and the Teaching of the Church

The covenant, the jubilee, and God's beloved poor

The Old Testament writers describe the great covenant of Sinai, which concretized the relationship of the community of Israel with God. This divine revelation illumines our understanding of the breadth and depth of charity.[11] In the covenant, God promises steadfast love and faithfulness to the people of Israel. They, in turn, pledge to worship him alone and to direct their lives in accordance with God's will, made explicit in Israel's great legal codes. Integral to those codes is the special concern charged to the community for the widows, orphans, and strangers who comprised God's beloved poor. While the poor remain faithful to God, they are oppressed by a combination of poverty, powerlessness, and exploitation by others. "What these groups of people have in common is their vulnerability and lack of power. They are often alone and have no protector or advocate."[12] The poor are oppressed politically and denied a decent share in the blessings of God's creation, which are intended to be shared by all of humanity.[13]

WHAT IS BIBLICAL JUSTICE?

"Biblical Justice is more comprehensive than subsequent philosophical definitions. It is not concerned with a strict definition of rights and duties, but with the rightness of the human condition before God and within society. Nor is justice opposed to love; rather, it is both a manifestation of love and a condition for love to grow. Because God loves Israel, he rescues them from oppression and summons them to be a people that 'does justice' and loves kindness. The quest for justice arises from loving gratitude for the saving acts of God and manifests itself in wholehearted love of God and neighbor" (National Conference of Catholic Bishops, *Economic Justice for All: Pastoral Letter on Catholic Social Teaching and the U.S. Economy* [Washington, D.C.: United States Catholic Conference, 1986], no. 39). Additionally, biblical justice provides deeper insight into the revelation and teaching of Jesus of Nazareth.

The jubilee year (cf. Lv 25), which fell every fifty years, was meant to restore equality among all the children of Israel, "offering new possibilities to families which had lost their property and even their personal freedom."[14] The jubilee year was proclaimed to assist those in need, to free those enslaved (often for debt), to restore property to its original owners, and to allow the poor to share fully in God's abundant blessings.

The call to jubilee was not aimed so much at the poor as it was at the rich. The rich were called to participate fully in the covenant by forgiving debts, returning land, and freeing slaves. Proclaiming jubilee was a requirement of just government, and the jubilee year was meant to restore social justice among the people. In doing so, it followed the tradition that those who possessed goods such as personal property were really only stewards charged with working for the good of all in the name of God, the sole owner of creation. God willed that these goods should serve everyone in a just way.

Jesus, jubilee, and God's love

In His teaching, Jesus inaugurated the great dual command to love God and neighbor passionately; this love forms the basis of all Christian morality.[15] Jesus illustrated this command with the parable of the compassionate Samaritan who interrupts his journey to come to the aid of a dying man by the roadside. "In this parable compassion is the bridge between mere seeing and action; love is made real through effective action."[16] The Beatitudes (Mt 5:1-12; Lk 6:20-23) tell us that the reign of God belongs to the poor and lowly and to those who stand with the poor, show mercy to them, and hunger and thirst for justice.

At the beginning of His public ministry, Jesus returned to the synagogue in Nazareth and read from the prophet Isaiah:

> *The Spirit of the Lord is upon me,*
> *because he has anointed me*
> *to bring glad tidings to the poor.*
> *He has sent me to proclaim liberty to captives*
> *and recovery of sight to the blind,*
> *to let the oppressed go free,*
> *and to proclaim a year acceptable to the Lord.* (Lk 4:18-19)

Jesus himself is the proclamation of the Great Jubilee. "Today," He added, "this scripture passage is fulfilled in your hearing" (Lk 4:21). In the fullness of time, it is Jesus who proclaims the good news to the poor. It is Jesus who gives sight to the blind and frees the oppressed. By His words and above all by His actions, Jesus ushered in a "year of the Lord's favor," becoming in His passion and death the ransom for many (Mk 10:45). "The Jubilee, a 'year of the Lord's favor,' characterizes all the activity of Jesus."[17]

In His ministry, Jesus healed the sick and disabled, returning them to good health and to their families and communities. He thus embodies the compassion of God and sets relationships right within the community. In all His encounters, "Jesus affirms and proclaims an essential equality of dignity among all human beings, men and women, whatever their ethnic origin, nation, or race, culture, political membership or social condition."[18]

Near the end of His earthly life, Jesus offered to His disciples a dramatic picture of the last judgment (Mt 25:31-46). All the nations of the world are assembled before the Son of Man, who divides them into those who are blessed by God forever and those who are cursed into eternal punishment. "The blessed are those who fed the hungry, gave drink to the thirsty, welcomed the stranger, clothed the naked, and visited the sick and imprisoned; the cursed are those who neglected these works of mercy and love."[19] Both the blessed and the cursed are shocked that they are judged according to their works of charity. Their shock increases when they find that in caring for or neglecting the poor, the hungry, the imprisoned, and the oppressed, they in fact were caring for or neglecting Jesus himself. Jesus, the embodiment of God's love, is to be found in those most in need. By rejecting them, we reject God made manifest in history.[20] By loving them, we remain in the God who is love, and God remains in us (1 Jn 4:16).

Inspired by the Spirit, the early Christian community shared the goods of creation with one another according to their needs (Acts 2:44, 4:32-34). All were urged to care for the widow and orphan (Jas 1:27) and the needs of others (Jas 2:16). The rich were warned sternly about the dangers of wealth and injustice toward their employees (Jas 5:1-6). In addition, seven deacons were chosen to ensure that the needs of poor widows and orphans were met and that justice was served within the community (Acts 6:1-7).

Acting in the name of charity and justice

No man or woman of good will should stand as an idle witness to the complex social problems of our day. Equally deserving of our attention and care is the private suffering of countless children, women, and men who do not have enough food to eat; who are deprived of adequate education, housing, or employment; or who suffer the trauma of abuse or neglect. The Fathers of the Second Vatican Council strongly urged a proactive response to these and other human sufferings: "This social order requires constant improvement. It must be founded on truth, built on justice and animated by love; in freedom it should grow every day toward a more human balance."[21]

JUSTICE AND CHARITY—PILLARS OF THE LIFE OF FAITH

One cannot ignore the demands of either charity or justice in the practice of the faith. Our Catholic teaching and tradition tell us that both of these virtues are complementary, inter-dependent, and divinely inspired.

Pope John Paul II cautioned us to practice justice that is inspired by charity: "Justice can reduce differences, eliminate discrimination and ensure the conditions necessary for respect for the dignity of the person. Justice, however, needs a soul. And the soul of justice is charity, a charity which places itself at the service of every person" (Address to UNIV Conference, Vatican City, March 31, 1999).

In his encyclical letter *The Gospel of Life* (*Evangelium Vitae*), Pope John Paul II reminds us that when life is challenged by hardship, sickness, and rejection, programs sponsored by the Church and others can stand as "eloquent expressions of what charity is able to devise in order to give everyone new reasons for hope and practical possibilities for life."[22]

Frequently, people are tempted to blame the poor for the conditions that oppress them. "It will be necessary above all to abandon a mentality in which the poor—as individuals and as peoples—are considered a burden, as irksome intruders trying to consume what others have produced."[23] Such a mentality plagues our present times, leading to a culture of death, which includes abortion, infanticide, euthanasia, assisted suicide, and capital punishment.

In the Christian life, no distinction can be made between the giver and the receiver. Even when it appears that one person provides a service and the other receives the benefits of that service, the "giver" often receives the most benefit from such acts of charity.[24] Thus, in 1995, during his pastoral visit to the United States, Pope John Paul II described a society "truly worthy of the human person" as one "in which none are so poor that they have nothing to give and none are so rich that they have nothing to receive."[25]

Pope John Paul II asks us to replace our fear and prejudice toward the poor with new attitudes for a Christian response: "Our support and promotion of human life must be accomplished through the *service of charity*, which finds expression in personal witness, various forms of volunteer work, social activity and political commitment."[26]

In recent years, charity has often been perceived negatively. Those who undertake charitable activities are seen as well-meaning "do-gooders" who actually foster dependency. Those who receive charity are treated in a demeaning manner. Even the word "charity" has been transformed by some into a derogatory term. We reject this characterization. In fact, Pope John Paul II cautioned us against a rejection of charity because of a "distorted" notion of justice: "The experience of the past and of our own time demonstrates that justice alone is not enough . . . if that deeper power, which is love, is not allowed to shape human life in its various dimensions."[27]

Throughout the Catholic teaching and tradition, we have seen the virtues of charity and justice presented as interdependent and complementary. Individual acts of assistance to and the sharing of goods with the needy are understood as expressions of charity, justice, or both. The *Catechism of the Catholic Church* teaches that "Charity is the greatest social commandment. It respects others and their rights. . . . Charity inspires a life of self-giving."[28]

In his apostolic exhortation *The Church in America* (*Ecclesia in America*), Pope John Paul II clearly presents the Christian responsibility to ensure that charity and justice result in individual actions and work for systemic change. We Christians must "reflect the attitude of Jesus, who came to 'proclaim Good News to the poor' (Lk 4:18). . . . This constant dedication to the poor and disadvantaged emerges in the Church's social teaching, which ceaselessly invites the Christian community to a commitment to overcome every form of exploitation and oppression. It is a question not only of alleviating the most serious and urgent needs through individual actions here and there, but of uncovering the roots of evil and proposing initiatives to make social, political and economic structures more just and fraternal."[29]

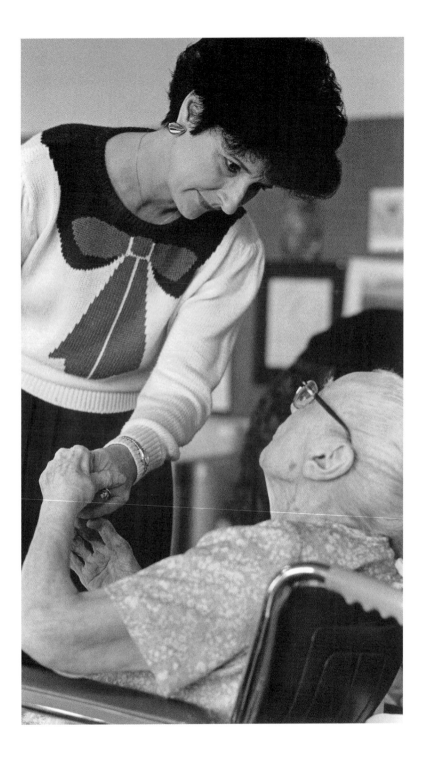

IV

Who Can and Should Respond to the Call for Charity and Justice?

All baptized persons

In our message *Everyday Christianity: To Hunger and Thirst for Justice*,[30] we emphasized that social justice and the common good are daily built up or torn down by the decisions and choices that we all make in every facet of our lives. As family members, workers, owners, managers, investors, consumers, and citizens, we are called to use our talents and resources in the service of others. We must build institutions across society that protect human life and dignity and promote justice and peace.

Powerful social, economic, and cultural forces encourage us to retreat from our neighbor into lifestyles of individualism, excessive consumption, and "me-first" politics. The Gospel, in contrast, urges us to be persons for others, deeply committed to the well-being of all members of the human family. As Pope John Paul II has made clear, the solidarity animated by charity "is not a feeling of vague compassion or shallow distress at the misfortunes of so many people, both near and far. On the contrary, it is a *firm and*

HOW DO WE GET STARTED IN THE WORK OF CHARITY, JUSTICE, AND PEACE?

We recommend two steps:

1.   Reach out to a person in need: tutor a child; visit a frail or sick elder; provide transportation to a disabled person; befriend a troubled teenager; babysit for young parents; or work in a parish food pantry or soup kitchen. These actions help to put a name and face to Christ among the poor, transforming the helper.

2.   Make one social issue your special concern, whether that be defense of life at all stages, hunger, homelessness, family violence, landmines, international debt relief, HIV/AIDS, criminal justice reform, or poverty. Study this topic; join a concerned church or civic group working on this issue; become active in a diocesan-sponsored legislative network; write to members of Congress or local elected officials; and vote responsibly.

persevering determination to commit oneself to the *common good*; that is to say to the good of all and of each individual, because we are all really responsible for *all*."[31]

It is too easy to be immobilized by the complexity of social problems, the feelings of exhaustion in the face of endless human needs, or the seeming powerlessness of one person to change the world. Yet one of the wonderful lessons of the Gospel is the power of the few to be leaven for many—the continuous wonder of planting small seeds from which great forests grow. By our own efforts, each of us can make the reign of God a reality.[32] Additionally, the poor themselves have a duty to develop their own resources, to work industriously, and to contribute to the good of society.

In recounting its history of social ministry, the Church can rejoice in the countless baptized women and men whose commitment to the poor and needy transformed their generation and inspired others with their dedication to service and justice; these women and men have felt joy in knowing Christ among the poor.

Families

Families are the first to know about and respond to the needs of their own members who cannot care for themselves. Sick children or elders, family members with disabilities or addictions, unemployed brothers or sisters, and others with special problems or needs are the first to receive the resources of their own families. Families are also the first schools of compassion and mercy, of solidarity and justice. It is in the

THE FAMILY IS THE BASIC UNIT OF SOCIETY

"The family has vital and organic links with society since it is its foundation and nourishes it continually through its role of service to life" (John Paul II, *On the Family* [*Familiaris Consortio*] [Washington, D.C.: United States Catholic Conference, 1982], no. 42).

home that children learn about their responsibility to family members and to the common good of the larger society and the world's needy.

Parents can best teach their children action for charity and justice by their own words and deeds. In the Christian home, children can learn compassion for families who are poor and needy and can begin to understand the personal and systemic causes of poverty and injustice. For children, the involvement of parents in parish social ministry activities or volunteer service to the poor and needy (with Catholic Charities or other organizations) represents an eloquent lesson in the Gospel's call to love and mercy. We encourage families to participate in Catholic Relief Services' Operation Rice Bowl, the Catholic Campaign for Human Development's Journey to Justice Process, and other Church-sponsored social ministry programs. Finally, parents should be the first to teach their children that advocacy for justice is intrinsic to Gospel-based charity and that "true charity leads to advocacy."[33]

Parishes

We addressed the social mission of the parish in our 1993 letter *Communities of Salt and Light*. There we offered basic resources to pastors, parish leaders, and parishioners who seek to strengthen the social ministry of their parishes. This was not a new teaching nor a new national program; rather, we provided an overall orientation and general framework for parish social ministry drawn from Catholic social teaching and local pastoral experience. In *Called to Global Solidarity* (1998), we urged parishes to reach beyond their own boundaries to extend the Gospel, to serve those in need, and to work for global justice and peace in all parts of the world.

While many steps have been taken across the country to enrich and carry out the social mission of our parishes, much more remains to be done. Our social tradition remains unknown to many parishioners, and parish social ministry remains the task for too few. As social conditions worsen and poverty deepens in a way unseen by most of us, parishes are called to greater consciousness as well as more determined action at home and abroad. We urge pastors, staff, and volunteers to be sensitive to the social mission of the Church in prayer and worship, preaching and education, support for parishioners' daily lives and work, outreach and charity, legislative action and community organizing, and global solidarity. We also urge parish leaders and members to develop links with diocesan Catholic Charities agencies, diocesan offices for justice and peace, the Catholic Campaign for Human Development, Catholic Relief Services, and Migration and Refugee Services in order to enhance service and advocacy at the parish, diocesan, national, and international levels. Catholic Charities agencies and other diocesan social ministries must reach out to parishes in order to support their social concerns activities and outreach.

The greatest gift that we have received from the Lord Jesus is the Eucharist: "Whoever eats this bread will live forever; and the bread that I will give is my flesh for the life of the world" (Jn 6:51). This gift is not meant to be hidden or hoarded. As the parish gathers for the celebration of the Eucharist, the needs and rights of the poor and disenfranchised must be placed on the table. The Council Fathers reminded us that "this Eucharistic celebration, to be full and sincere, ought to lead on the one hand to the various works of charity and mutual help, and on the other hand to missionary activity and the various forms of Christian witness."[34] The Word proclaimed in the Eucharist must affirm and celebrate the parish's work for charity, justice, and peace. The Word must inspire social analysis and concerted action, leading the people of God to a renewed commitment to the poor.

Religious congregations

The work of charity has a distinguished history among numerous religious orders in this country and around the world. Their continuing commitment is a beautiful witness to the centrality of the work for charity, justice, peace, and solidarity at the heart of Gospel-inspired lives. For our faith to be expressed vibrantly in decades to come, such congregations and organizations must continue in service to the needy, as advocates for justice and peace and as vehicles for the involvement of Catholics and others. Their

A HISTORY OF LOVING SERVICE TO THOSE MOST IN NEED

By the year 1900, the organized response of the Catholic community in the United States to social needs included more than 800 Catholic charitable institutions. Ten years later, in 1910, 445 Catholic orphanages and institutions were caring for 88,860 dependent children. By 1919, the Sisters of Charity and the Daughters of Charity operated sixty-two maternity hospitals, infant homes, and orphanages, and cared for 10,653 infants and children. Sisters of the Good Shepherd cared for 7,036 delinquent and neglected girls in fifty-eight institutions. Sisters in more than forty other congregations cared for another 41,000 infants and children. Religious priests and brothers cared for 4,900 in their protectories, industrial schools, and orphanages.

Source: Dorothy M. Brown and Elizabeth McKeown, *The Poor Belong to Us: Catholic Charities and American Welfare* (Cambridge, Mass.: Harvard University, 1997), 5

work on behalf of people is a testament to the power of the Gospel and to the needs of people in communities across this nation and the world.

Beginning in 1727 with the Ursuline Sisters in New Orleans, women and men religious served waves of immigrants arriving on American shores. These religious reached out to the Native Americans who were unjustly and forcibly removed from their lands and to the African Americans who were brought here against their will under the horrible and tragic system of slavery. Throughout the history of the United States, religious—especially communities of religious women—provided leadership and staffing for Church-sponsored agencies and institutions that served the most vulnerable members of society.

While the institutional character of the Catholic social commitment has changed remarkably over the past century, and while the number of men and women in religious congregations has declined, the commitment of women and men religious to the poor has continued. Their own vows of poverty are signs to society of their commitment to the poor. Their social ministry efforts within the United States include residential institutions, in-home services, schools for needy and poor students, service in and leadership of diocesan Catholic Charities agencies, counseling, parish-based social ministries, adult education, community centers, community organizing, justice and peace centers, health-related services,[35] and foundations for funding social services and advocacy.

Lay associations

Lay associations have grown in number over the past century, have diversified in service to the poor and needy, and have worked as advocates for justice and peace. The National Council of Catholic Women, the Society of St. Vincent de Paul, the Ladies of Charity, and the Christ Child Society, to name just a few, work with children and families in need, provide assistance during natural disasters, train volunteers for social service, advocate for and

THE NATIONAL COUNCIL OF CATHOLIC WOMEN

Founded in 1920, the National Council of Catholic Women (NCCW) is a federation of more than 6,000 Catholic women's organizations in 115 dioceses in the United States. Its membership includes parish-based groups, diocesan councils of Catholic women, and national organizations such as the Catholic Daughters of the Americas, the Daughters of Isabella, and the Ladies Auxiliary of the Knights of Peter Claver. After a long history of social ministry across the United States, NCCW includes the following among its current activities:

- Respite programs in thirty dioceses to provide relief to family caregivers for the frail elderly
- 19 mentoring programs for at-risk pregnant women
- A nationwide program of education, awareness, and support services for victims of domestic violence
- Volunteer work at local soup kitchens and in resettlement programs for refugees and immigrants
- Outreach to women in prison and their children
- Support of overseas programs for women and children in developing countries

with the seemingly powerless and voiceless, and work to educate Catholics and the broader society about their responsibilities to the common good.

During the latter half of the twentieth century, a number of religious congregations, dioceses, state Catholic conferences, Catholic colleges and universities, and lay movements have initiated dynamic and creative lay volunteer programs to serve the needy and to advocate justice. These volunteers teach in inner-city schools, assist in Catholic Charities and other diocesan offices, staff food banks, engage in community organizing, facilitate legislative networks, and serve in overseas relief and development programs. In 1997, 5,500 full-time volunteers were offering such services in the United States and many hundreds of others were working abroad.

THE SOCIETY OF ST. VINCENT DE PAUL

In 1833, the Society of St. Vincent de Paul was founded in France by Blessed Frederic Ozanam; in 1845, it was established in St. Louis, Mo. The society has led women and men to grow spiritually by offering person-to-person service to the needy and suffering in the tradition of its patron, St. Vincent de Paul, the "Apostle of Charity" and "Father of the Poor."

The society numbers 64,521 volunteers, who annually serve 5.5 million people at 4,986 sites. The society operates 2,123 special works, 642 stores, 530 diocesan councils, and 343 district councils. The society sees the connection between charity and justice in terms expressed by Blessed Frederic Ozanam: "The order of society is based on two virtues: justice and charity. However, justice presupposes a lot of love already, for one needs to love a person a great deal in order to respect his or her rights which restrict our rights, and his or her liberty which restricts our liberty. Justice has its limits whereas charity knows none" (Frederic Ozanam, *The History of Civilization*, vol. II, trans. by Ashley C. Glyn, 1868).

The society includes in its current goals a re-commitment to works of advocacy in defense of the powerless and the voiceless.

THE LADIES OF CHARITY

In 1617, the Ladies of Charity was founded in France by St. Vincent de Paul and St. Louise de Marillac, the patroness of social workers. It was first established in the United States in St. Louis, Mo., in 1875 by Catherine Harkins. The Ladies of Charity offer services through seventy-six local associations and come from 900 parishes in twenty-three states.

During their U.S. history, the Ladies of Charity have staffed houses for orphaned girls, found jobs for the unemployed, paid rent, visited the sick, provided foster homes for unwed mothers, and raised resources for domestic missions and overseas relief. Their mission includes performing works of charity, addressing the problems of poverty and injustice to improve the quality of life for all, and fostering civic cooperation for the relief of the poor and the betterment of social conditions.

THE CHRIST CHILD SOCIETY

Founded in 1887, in Washington, D.C., by Mary Virginia Merrick, the Christ Child Society's objective was ". . .to clothe the children under the age of twelve years whose parents were unable to do so and to give the little ones a Happy Christmas."

Today, with more than 7,000 members in thirty-eight chapters across the United States, this non-profit organization provides clothing, mental and physical health services, education and recreation activities, shelter, and a variety of diverse programs to under-served children regardless of race or creed.

In the new century, communities will continue to look to the Christ Child Society for spiritual, financial, material, and volunteer assistance from our Catholic associations that embrace members of all denominations, expressing their love of the Christ Child by service to God's children.

With the vast array of organizations working on various aspects of the social ministry of the Church, it is important to stress the need for collaboration and cooperation at the local, diocesan, national, and international levels. With escalating needs and often diminishing resources, the power of collaborative approaches to problems of poverty and injustice cannot be underestimated. In addition, the bonds of charity that call us to reach out to those in need should be manifest in our working with one another in service of the same Gospel.

Dioceses

Social ministry is an expression of the Gospel and of the prophetic, servant ministry of Jesus Christ; as such, it is a fundamental element of the mission of the Church. The responsibility for social ministry was discussed by the 1985 Extraordinary Synod of Bishops: "Following the Second Vatican Council, the Church became more aware of her mission in the service of

NATIONAL CONFERENCE OF CATHOLIC CHARITIES

The first meetings of the National Conference of Catholic Charities (NCCC) took place at The Catholic University of America. Catholic schools of social work have played a crucial role in preparing those engaged in Catholic Charities work.

From 1969 to 1972, in the wake of the Second Vatican Council, the "War on Poverty," and the tumultuous events of the 1960s, NCCC members undertook a theological reflection on their identity, mission, and activities. At that time, they recognized their rootedness in the Church as a faith-based movement that affirmed its commitment to provide quality service in response to the needs of local communities and in collaboration with those in need of assistance. They re- captured their historical role in social action to transform the social order. They undertook a leadership role in convening people of good will to reflect prayerfully on those influences in the culture that promote or undermine human dignity. Diocesan Catholic Charities agencies were urged to reach out to parishes to engage parishioners in collaborative efforts to initiate parish- based social ministry to promote charity and justice.

the poor, the oppressed, and the outcast. In this preferential option, which must not be understood as exclusive, the true spirit of the Gospel shines forth."[36] Parishes, dioceses, religious institutes, and lay associations employ various structures to deliver such ministries. The diocesan bishop provides leadership for these ministries, in keeping with the promise made at his ordination, "to show compassion and kindness for the sake of the Lord's name to the poor, to strangers, and to all who are in need."[37]

The diocese often extends its works of charity and justice through its Catholic Charities agency. At the turn of the century, while local pastors struggled to fulfill the temporal as well as spiritual needs of parishioners, bishops began to formalize the apostolate of charity by establishing diocesan Catholic Charities agencies and working closely with other social apostolates sponsored by religious orders and lay associations. These bishops saw the need for professional training for those engaged in Catholic

Charities work. In 1910, the National Conference of Catholic Charities, later renamed Catholic Charities USA, was established as a forum for continuing education, networking, and advocacy.

We take this opportunity to extend our heartfelt gratitude and encouragement to those countless individuals who, over the years, have been engaged in Catholic Charities service at the parish, diocesan, and national levels. In 1997, 47,532 staff and 262,622 volunteers and board members helped to make Catholic Charities the largest voluntary social service network in the United States. Among the services they provided were the following:

- 6.8 million people were offered emergency services, such as food, shelter, financial assistance, clothing, medication, and domestic disaster-response assistance.
- 3.8 million people were extended social services in order to become self-sufficient; these services included social support, counseling, education and family support, health services, housing, immigration services and refugee resettlement, HIV/AIDS care, and pregnancy and adoption services.[38]
- 1,617 community programs were sponsored, 49 percent of which were neighborhood or parish organizations, 13 percent were cooperatives, and 13 percent were housing corporations.
- 89 percent of Catholic Charities agencies reported active social policy advocacy at the national, state, and local levels, with the top five national issues being: income security and welfare reform; international justice and refugees; economy, employment, and minimum wage; hunger and nutrition; and abortion.

We recall the words of Pope John Paul II, spoken in 1987, when he addressed the assembled representatives of Catholic Charities USA and other Church-sponsored social service agencies: "Gather, transform, and serve! When done in the name of Jesus Christ, this is the spirit of Catholic Charities and of all who work in this cause, because it is the faithful following of the one who 'did not come to be served but to serve' (Mk 10:45). By working for a society which fosters the dignity of every human person, not only are you serving the poor, but you are renewing the founding vision of this nation under God! And may God reward you abundantly!"[39] *We strongly appeal to our diocesan and parish communities to support the activities and form partnerships with Catholic Charities.*

As bishops, we recognize the need for Catholic Charities to develop professional and specialized competency in the diverse fields of human and social services. We urge these agencies to respect the cultural and faith traditions of those they serve and to collaborate actively with Catholic health care and education apostolates and with human service organizations sponsored by other faith communities. We also want to thank the many staff and volunteers of other faith traditions who generously bring their own commitment to the poor and needy and thereby enrich the work of Catholic social agencies across the country.

It is equally important, however, for Catholic agencies to preserve and promote their Catholic roots, identity, and mission. This needs to be done by sponsoring education and ongoing formation for board members, staff, and volunteers in the Church's faith and moral teaching. In keeping with this teaching, agencies and organizations should be exemplary in providing fair salaries and comprehensive benefits to their employees, as well as maintaining appropriate support systems for their volunteers. It is also important for agency leaders, staff, and volunteers to engage in dialogue with bishops, priests, deacons, religious, and lay pastoral leaders and to share information and opportunities for service with all the Catholic faithful.

The strong and effective thirty-year history of the Catholic Campaign for Human Development convinces us that community organizing, community-based economic development, and education for social change must be integral components of a wider range of Catholic social ministries. The "cries of those who are poor" in our society demand new and renewed commitment to systemic social change through organizing, community outreach, legislative networks, racial reconciliation, social policy development, coalition-building, and public and private sector partnerships for economic development. Provisions for social services alone cannot affect the permanent, broad, and deep changes in society that are rightfully wanted and needed by those living in poverty; these changes are needed so that the poor might achieve the freedom and dignity consistent with gospel love.[40]

The universal Church
and the global human family

In the beginning of our 1986 pastoral letter on economic justice, we observed that "*beyond our own shores, the reality of 800 million people living in absolute poverty and 450 million malnourished or facing starvation casts an ominous shadow over all these hopes and problems at home.*"[41]

On behalf of the U.S. Catholic community, Catholic Relief Services (CRS) serves millions of poor people all over the world. By responding to victims of disasters, supporting community self-help projects, promoting innovative peace and reconciliation initiatives, and contributing to more just societies, CRS provides opportunities for people who have no political voice, no economic power, and no social status. In more than eighty countries, CRS provides active expressions of Christ's love in the world and strengthens the local Catholic Church's ability to serve the poor and to advocate justice.

CRS also provides a variety of programs in partnership with dioceses, parishes, organizations, and individuals to promote understanding, awareness, and solidarity with poor people throughout the world.

Both CRS and Catholic Charities USA participate actively with Catholic social service and development agencies from more than 160 countries throughout the world in the Confederation of Caritas Internationalis. These organizations often constitute the first line of response in many of the world's natural and human-made disasters, and they just as frequently join those affected and the local Catholic church in the difficult work of long-term development.

Recent decades have seen an unprecedented movement of people throughout the world. Much of the disruption of peoples has been caused by political unrest, suppression of human rights, ethnic cleansing, and abject poverty. Migration and Refugee Services of the United States Catholic Conference, in partnership with diocesan Catholic Charities agencies, has been on the cutting edge of refugee assistance through the resettlement and citizenship process. New citizens, by the hundreds of thousands, have been welcomed by these efforts. This is a testimony to our solidarity with the poor and disenfranchised.

We cannot reflect upon the gospel duty of love, therefore, without an honest recognition of the ever-worsening problems of the world around us and an acknowledgment that charity, as Pope Paul VI stated, must now be worldwide: "The rule according to which in the past those were to be helped who are more closely bound to us now applies to all who are in need throughout the world."[42] This means that individuals, parishes, and organizations must reach out to other nations and to their poor in ways that would emphasize the North-South solidarity of the entire North American continent. *Twinning of parishes and diocesan agencies, support for Catholic Relief Services and the American Bishops' Overseas Appeal, mission efforts, migration and refugee activities, advocacy on international issues, and other global ministries are signs of solidarity in a shrinking and suffering world,*[43] *signs of the charity of the Gospel.*

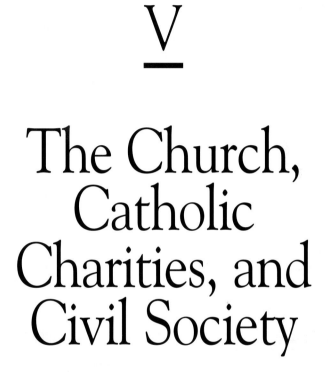

V

The Church, Catholic Charities, and Civil Society

The charitable and justice-oriented activities of the Church are integral to the collective responsibility of all citizens to build the common good of our nation and of the entire human family. In his 1979 visit to our country, Pope John Paul II said, "Catholics of the United States, while developing your own legitimate institutions, you also participate in the nation's affairs within the framework of institutions and organizations springing from the nation's common history and from your common concern. This you do hand in hand with your fellow citizens of every creed and confession."[44]

To promote the common good, we Catholics have the right and the responsibility to join all members of society to improve the conditions of the human family. We have a corresponding obligation to promote and uphold the sacredness and integrity of human life at all stages from conception to natural death.[45] In our society, we exercise our responsibility toward the common good by actively participating in the voluntary, private, and public sectors of civil society.

The voluntary sector

One of the strengths of U.S. society is the willingness of millions of Americans to join together in literally hundreds of thousands of civic organizations or associations to address local needs. These mediating institutions often focus on meeting the needs of youth, the elderly, persons with disabilities, and the poor. Catholics continue to be active members and leaders of such civic organizations, in addition to organizations sponsored directly by the Church.

In keeping with the Catholic social principle of *subsidiarity*,[46] such memberships are to be encouraged as ways for Catholics and others to exercise their call to charity, justice, peace, and solidarity. Voluntary organizations play an important part in our collective efforts to promote the common good, protect human life, reach out to people in need, and work for a more just and compassionate society.

Parishes, diocesan organizations, and Catholic charity and justice organizations should take every reasonable opportunity to work with such associations as well as with those organizations sponsored by other faith communities. Participation in community-wide workplace efforts and other fund-raising campaigns, such as the United Way and the Combined Federal Campaign, has been of great value in the past. Our participation in such funding efforts should be characterized in each instance by respect for our religious and ethical values, and should result in fair and equitable support for Catholic social service efforts. This practical ecumenism and civic collaboration can enhance the work of Catholic organizations, meet needs that could not otherwise be met, and strengthen the bonds of charity across society.

The private sector

In responding to the needs of the poor and others, corporations, businesses, and unions can play a strong role. As we have repeatedly indicated, *"The first line of attack against poverty must be to build and sustain a healthy economy that provides employment opportunities at just wages for all adults who are able to work."*[47] Work provides a decent livelihood for families, lifts many out of poverty, and eliminates the need for charity in all but emergency circumstances. In keeping with this priority, employers and unions must ensure that jobs provide living wages and adequate benefits.[48]

In addition, many private-sector organizations have provided volunteers, financial support, and expertise to church organizations and civic associations in service to the needy and in support of advocacy for better community and public responses. However, in the face of escalating social problems, these resources are needed more than ever. As charities grapple with more complex issues and with the need for productive employment, businesses and labor organizations can supply additional resources—technical assistance, business skills, and capital—to support more creative responses, such as domestic and overseas micro-enterprise loan programs, cooperative development, and construction and rehabilitation of housing.

The public sector

Our Catholic tradition teaches that the moral function of government is to protect human rights and secure basic justice for all members of the commonwealth.[49] Society as a whole and in all its subsidiary parts is responsible for building up the common good and for responding to the needs of the poor and vulnerable. But government is responsible for guaranteeing that the minimum conditions for social activity, including both human rights and justice, are met. This responsibility includes generating employment and establishing fair labor practices, guaranteeing the economy's infrastructure, regulating trade and commerce, and levying the taxes to carry out its duties.[50]

How society responds to the needs of the poor through its public policies serves as the litmus test for whether it conforms to the demands of justice and charity. The Church has long supported minimum wage and fair labor standards as essential for the protection of workers. For those who cannot find fair wages or cannot work due to age, disability, parental responsibilities, or another cause, the economic safety net must be ensured by government insurance and income support systems. "The programs that make up this system should serve the needs of the poor in a manner that respects their dignity and provides adequate support."[51]

Catholic social teaching assigns a positive role for government in social welfare. Thus the Fathers of the Second Vatican Council declared that "the growing complexity of modern situations makes it necessary for public authority to intervene more frequently in social, cultural and economic matters in order to achieve conditions more favorable to the free and effective pursuit by citizens and groups of the advancement of people's total well-being."[52] As a result of the Great Depression, which lasted from 1929 to 1941, it became evident to people of the United States that only the government could develop resources to ensure regular income support for aged, disabled, or otherwise needy families. It has accomplished this by establishing such vehicles as Social Security; retirement, disability, and survivors' programs; unemployment compensation; workers' compensation; food stamps; and dependent children programs.[53] No private charity has the resources, for example, to provide steady monthly support to families without adequate income. These beliefs and principles, however, have come under attack during the latter part of the twentieth century as a negative attitude developed with regard to the responsibility of government to develop the policies and programs that make it possible for all people to fulfill their basic human needs.

The U.S. government has also provided funding for needed social services by purchasing service contracts and providing other funding for nonprofit agencies. These agencies, in turn, have provided hands-on care by trained staff, enrichment of volunteers, private fund raising, and dedicated commitment to deliver the services to children, families, elders, and people with disabilities. This pluralism has been an essential characteristic of twentieth-century social service delivery in the United States. Pluralism in public programs is strengthened and made more genuine when individuals can choose to receive social services through a variety of providers, including religiously affiliated social service organizations.

As advocates for and contributors to the common good, Catholic social service agencies and other voluntary social service providers deserve acceptance, support, and respect from the public sector. Diversity of culture, values, and identities is widespread across this country and justifies providing different service models in different communities. The goal of serving a genuinely pluralistic society is best achieved by the participation of providers reflecting the diversity of our communities. In establishing partnerships with voluntary agencies, public sector authorities must not make requirements that weaken agency identities and integrity or undermine agency commitments to serve people in need. On the other hand, political entities that are primarily responsible for the common good should appropriately require accountability by Church-sponsored and other social agencies for standards of service and expenditures of public funds.

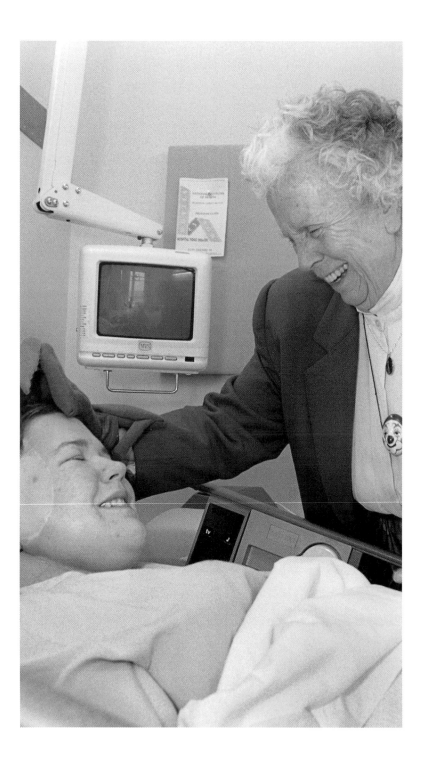

VI

Challenges of the New Millennium

Changing relationships between government and Church-sponsored services

For at least a century, religious and community-based nonprofit organizations have been providing social services under contracts with government at all levels. This system of joint responsibility has served children and families, communities, and society very well. In recent years, a new problem has arisen when legislators and public policy makers attempt to balance budgets by "outsourcing" social services to commercial enterprises; this is known as privatization. Responsibility for ensuring and managing resources to support social services is shifted first from the federal level, then to the state level. States shift responsibilities to localities, and states and localities often turn to the private sector in the name of greater efficiency, cost-effectiveness, and local control.

These public-private partnerships may help manifest *subsidiarity* by respecting the vital roles that non-governmental entities can play in providing social services. This is especially evident when seen in the context of *solidarity*, which commits us to the common good, with particular attention to the poor and needy. As we noted in our letter on economic justice, "The challenge of today is to move beyond abstract disputes about whether more or less government intervention is needed, to consideration of creative ways of enabling government and private groups to work together effectively."[54] The issue is not whether privatization is legitimate, but how best to selectively, fairly, and effectively implement it in ways that provide services to people in need while maintaining justice for those affected by privatization and protecting the rights of public- and private-sector employees.

Our public decision makers, legislators, and government administrators have the primary responsibility to ensure that the move to privatization does not turn into profiteering at the expense of the poor and vulnerable. Policy makers must require that the public good is the primary consideration for new arrangements in the social service arena. Catholic social

service providers and social justice advocates must make concerted efforts to ensure that government social service and benefit programs maximize service to needy families, protect their rights and interests, avoid any compromise that might threaten their basic mission and values, and, above all, promote the common good. Their advocacy efforts must be coordinated, wherever possible, with those of other religiously affiliated and civic agencies and with organizations of affected participants.

Lay leadership, staff, and volunteer support

One of the distinguishing characteristics of Catholic Charities and other Church-sponsored social services and justice advocacy programs is the presence of lay leadership, staffing, and volunteering. While religious largely led the social institutions of the early part of this century and priests led the diocesan Catholic Charities agencies at mid-century, lay women and men who are trained professionals have joined priests and religious in leading our social ministry organizations today. They have done so because they share the Church's concerns for charity and justice, solidarity and peace.

Because of the increasing responsibilities assumed by the laity and because of the many forces shaping and challenging their work for charity and justice, we urge agencies and organizations to make increased commitments to leadership formation, staff development, and volunteer support. Our tradition of Catholic social teaching, ethical heritage, and spirituality must be joined with training in leadership, organizational development, fund raising, professional skills, social analysis, and new technologies. This should be done not only with appreciation for the diverse religious backgrounds of those involved, but also with commitment to clear organizational mission and Catholic identity. If the social ministry of the Church is to grow in the twenty-first century in order to meet the needs of the poor and vulnerable, it will require a broadening and deepening of the preparation, support, and animation of the boards, staff, and volunteers who make charity, justice, peace, and solidarity a reality.

Since significant numbers of women and people of color are served by and are serving in Catholic social ministry programs, we must make determined efforts to recruit and retain women and people of color in organizational leadership.

Sharing the "Good News": Evangelization through the works of charity and justice

The most fundamental mission of the Church is to evangelize, that is, to "proclaim the good news of the kingdom of God" (Lk 4:43). Pope Paul VI explained this as follows: "Evangelizing is in fact the grace and vocation proper to the Church, her deepest identity."[55] He maintained that, in evangelization, one could not "ignore the importance of the problems so much discussed today, concerning justice, liberation, development and peace in the world. This would be to forget the lesson which comes to us from the Gospel concerning love of our neighbor who is suffering and in need."[56]

As we search for more meaningful participation in the Great Jubilee of the Year 2000 and in the third millennium, we recall the urgent opportunities before us to preach the message of Jesus through our good works of charity and justice. Pope John Paul II stresses the timeliness and necessity of such active witness to the Gospel: "Today more than ever, the Church is aware that her social message will gain credibility more immediately from the *witness of actions* than as a result of its internal logic and consistency."[57]

Inviting the participation of all Catholics and other people of good will

The social mission of our Church cannot and should not be fulfilled by only a small number of professionals, community organizers, or social activists. The barriers that prevent millions of women, men, and children in this country—and billions in other parts of the world—from being "treat[ed] like guests at your family table"[58] will be lifted only when all of us as believers in the good news of our Lord Jesus Christ are willing to put our faith into action.

Thus, in our message *Everyday Christianity*, we posed the following questions: "How do we connect worship on Sunday to work on Monday? How is the Gospel proclaimed not only in the pulpits of our parishes, but also in the everyday lives of Catholic people? How does the Church gathered on the Sabbath act as the people of God who are scattered and active every other day of the week? How can we best carry the values of our faith into family life, the marketplace, and the public square?"[59] *One way to invite Catholics to deepen their commitment to serve their neighbors in need is to promote the* Jubilee Pledge for Charity, Justice, and Peace: A Catholic Commitment for the New Millennium (*see back cover*).

VII

Conclusion

As teachers of the faith and as pastors, we share the burden and pain of all within our country and our world who suffer from physical illnesses, struggle with emotional problems, or experience firsthand the social ills of poverty, unemployment, discrimination, racism, and other forms of exclusion. With equally strong feelings, we celebrate Jesus' call to discipleship, the call expressed through the inspiring social ministry of the Church. Through the last two millennia, our forebears in the faith have included monks who tilled the land, men and women religious who founded hospitals and shelters for the poor, and women and men who have devoted themselves to the needy and to those on the margins of society. Our forebears performed these acts of service out of a deep conviction that Jesus' words "whatever you did for one of these least brothers of mine, you did for me" (Mt 25:40) were not intended to remain a pious wish, but were meant to become a concrete life commitment.[60]

Through our works of charity and justice, we Catholics are challenged to put into practice the principles that we have learned from our Church's teachings and tradition. Thus, in marking the one-hundredth anniversary of contemporary Catholic social teaching, Pope John Paul II called on us to consider the social message of the Gospel as not just a "theory, but above all else a basis and a motivation for action."[61]

Many Catholics have entered the mainstream of American society[62] and have made remarkable achievements in the political, social, and economic life of our nation. For some Catholics, this process of assimilation into the economic and social mainstream, however, has resulted in a widening split between our faith and our everyday choices. This phenomenon was labeled by the Fathers of the Second Vatican Council as one of "the most serious problems of our time."[63] While counting our blessings as Catholics, we cannot fail to hear Jesus' invitation to the wealthy and good young man to "go, sell what you have and give to [the] poor. . . . Then come, follow me" (Mt 19:21). How will we respond? Will we go away sad since we have many possessions? Or will we respond with generosity and selfless service by walking with those living in poverty? Pope John Paul II has stressed these same concerns and put them in a way which speaks to the human heart:

The Church has always proclaimed a love of preference for the poor. Perhaps the language is new, but the reality is not. Nor has the Church taken a narrow view of poverty and the poor. Poverty, certainly, is often a matter of material deprivation. But it is also a matter of spiritual impoverishment, the lack of human liberties and the result of any violation of human rights and dignity. . . .

The Christian view is that human beings are to be valued for what they are, not for what they have. In loving the poor and serving those in whatever need, the Church seeks above all to respect and heal their human dignity. The aim of Christian solidarity and service is to defend and promote, in the name of Jesus Christ, the dignity and fundamental human rights of every person.[64]

Let us greet the new millennium in the spirit of charity and justice by asking God for the grace and enlightenment of the Holy Spirit to make a place at our family table for all, especially for those who are the "least" among us, and to face the pastoral challenge before us: **in all things, charity.**

Notes

1. John Paul II, *On the Coming of the Third Millennium* (*Tertio Millennio Adveniente*) (TMA) (Washington, D.C.: United States Catholic Conference, 1994), no. 13; cf. Subcommittee on the Third Millennium, National Conference of Catholic Bishops, *A Parish Guide to the Jubilee Year 2000: Open Wide the Doors to Christ* (Washington, D.C.: United States Catholic Conference, 1999).

2. John Paul II, *Bull of Indiction of the Great Jubilee of the Year 2000* (*Incarnationis Mysterium*) (Washington, D.C.: United States Catholic Conference, 1999), no. 12.

3. Cf. Second Vatican Council, *Pastoral Constitution on the Church in the Modern World* (*Gaudium et Spes*) (GS), no. 41, in *Vatican Council II: The Conciliar and Post Conciliar Documents, New Revised Edition*, ed. Austin Flannery, 2 vols. (Northport, N.Y.: Costello Publishing Company, 1996): "The Gospel . . . never ceases to encourage the employment of human talents in the service of God and humanity, and, finally, it commends everyone to the charity of all."

4. Centre Catholique International de Genève, *Informations Internationales*, no. 218, October 1998.

5. John Paul II, *The Church in America* (*Ecclesia in America*) (EA) (Washington, D.C.: United States Catholic Conference, 1999), no. 56.

6. Ibid.

7. Catholic Charities USA, *Responding to Welfare Reform: A Report from Catholic Charities USA* (Alexandria, Va.: Catholic Charities USA, September 1998), pp. 11-12.

8. Charles M. A. Clark, "A Basic Income for the United States of America: Ensuring That the Benefits of Economic Progress Are Equitably Shared," in *The Vincentian Chair of Social Justice Presentations* (Jamaica, N.Y.: St. John's University, 1997), 38.

9. Vatican Congregation for Catholic Education, *Guidelines for the Study and Teaching of the Church's Social Doctrine in the Formation of Priests* (Vatican City: Libreria Editrice Vaticana, 1989), no. 1.

10. Ibid.

11. National Conference of Catholic Bishops, *Economic Justice for All: Pastoral Letter on Catholic Social Teaching and the U.S. Economy* (Washington, D.C.: United States Catholic Conference, 1986), nos. 35-40.

12. Ibid., no. 38.

13. Cf. TMA, no. 13: "If in his Providence God had given the earth to humanity, that meant that he had given it to everyone. Therefore *the riches of Creation were to be considered as a common good of the whole of humanity*. Those who possessed these goods as personal property were really only stewards, ministers charged with working in the name of God, who remains the sole owner in the full sense, since it is God's will that created goods should serve everyone in a just way."

14. TMA, no. 13.

15. *Economic Justice for All*, no. 43.

16. Ibid.

17. TMA, no. 11.

18. Vatican Congregation for Catholic Education, *Guidelines for the Study and Teaching of the Church's Social Doctrine in the Formation of Priests* (Vatican City: Libreria Editrice Vaticana, 1989), no. 16.

19. *Economic Justice for All*, no. 44.

20. Ibid., no. 43.

21. GS, no. 26.

22. John Paul II, *The Gospel of Life* (*Evangelium Vitae*) (EV) (Washington, D.C.: United States Catholic Conference, 1995), no. 88.

23. John Paul II, *On the Hundredth Anniversary of Rerum Novarum* (*Centesimus Annus*) (CA) (Washington, D.C.: United States Catholic Conference, 1991), no. 28.

24. John Paul II, *Rich in Mercy* (*Dives in Misericordia*) (DM) (Vatican City: Libreria Editrice Vaticana, 1980), no. 14.

25. John Paul II, Homily in Giants Stadium, Archdiocese of Newark, in *Origins* 28:18 (October 8, 1995).

26. EV, no. 87.

27. DM, no. 12.

28. *Catechism of the Catholic Church* (CCC) (Washington, D.C.: United States Catholic Conference, 1994), no. 1889. Cf. also CCC, no. 2446, which quotes two statements of St. John Chrysostom: "Not to enable the poor to share in our goods is to steal from them and deprive them of life," and "The demands of justice must be satisfied first of all; that which is already due in justice is not to be offered as a gift of charity."

29. EA, no. 18.

30. National Conference of Catholic Bishops/United States Catholic Conference, *Everyday Christianity: To Hunger and Thirst for Justice* (Washington, D.C.: United States Catholic Conference, 1998).

31. John Paul II, *On Social Concern* (*Sollicitudo Rei Socialis*) (Washington, D.C.: United States Catholic Conference, 1987), no. 38.

32. Cf. *Economic Justice for All*, no. 119: "Volunteering time, talent, and money to work for greater justice is a fundamental expression of Christian love and social solidarity. All who have more than they need must come to the aid of the poor."

33. Ibid., no. 356. In *Cadre Study: Toward a Renewed Catholic Charities Movement* (Alexandria, Va: Catholic Charities USA, 1992 edition), 34, we find the following explanation of advocacy: "One integral component of social action is that of advocacy, the courageous calling of attention to the root causes of poverty and oppression. . . . In its broadest sense, the advocacy role must include a diligence in perceiving human needs . . . ; an openness towards those who do not share these conditions; a constant urging for correction of abuses; and a public pleading for truth, justice, and clarity. It also means assisting individuals and groups who seek a righting of the injustices afflicting them or a correction of the abuses to which they are subjected."

34. Second Vatican Council, *Decree on the Ministry and Life of Priests* (*Presbyterorum Ordinis*), no. 6, in *Vatican Council II: The Conciliar and Post Conciliar Documents, New Revised Edition*.

35. In several documents, we have addressed the Catholic health ministry as a separate, but related, ministry of the Church. Cf. *Health and Health Care* (1981) and *Ethical and Religious Directives for Catholic Health Care Services* (1994) (Washington, D.C.: United States Catholic Conference).

36. *Extraordinary Synod of Bishops* (1985), *Final Report*, D, 6.

37. *Rite of Ordination of a Bishop*, Promise of the Elect.

38. Catholic Charities USA, *Annual Survey Findings* (Alexandria, Va.: Catholic Charities USA, 1998). Report prepared by Flynn Research, Harpers Ferry, W. Va.

39. John Paul II, Address to the Representatives of Catholic Charities USA, San Antonio, Texas (September 13, 1987), in *Origins* 17:17 (October 8, 1987).

40. The 1981 Annual Survey of Catholic Charities USA reported that only one out of four people served needed emergency assistance, primarily food and shelter. This represented fewer than 1 million people. By 1997, members of Catholic Charities USA provided emergency assistance to 6.8 million people (two out of three of the 10.6 million seeking services from Catholic Charities)—this represents an astonishing 700 percent increase.

41. *Economic Justice for All*, no. 4.

42. Paul VI, *The Development of Peoples* (*Populorum Progressio*) (Washington, D.C.: United States Catholic Conference, 1967), no. 49.

43. National Conference of Catholic Bishops, *Communities of Salt and Light: Reflections on the Social Mission of the Parish* (Washington, D.C.: United States Catholic Conference, 1994), 10-11.

44. John Paul II, Address at Yankee Stadium (October 2, 1979), in *Justice in the Marketplace: Collected Statements of the Vatican and the U.S. Catholic Bishops on Economic Policy, 1881-1984* (Washington, D.C.: United States Catholic Conference, 1985), 350. Cf. also CCC, no. 1925, which delineates three essential elements of the common good: (1) respect for and promotion of the fundamental rights of the person; (2) prosperity or development of the spiritual and temporal goods of society; and (3) the peace and security of the group and its members.

45. In CA, no. 47, John Paul II expresses the caution that our basic Christian values should never be compromised nor manipulated in the name of collaborative efforts within society: "There is a growing inability to situate particular interests within the framework of a coherent vision of the common good. The latter is not simply the sum total of particular interests; rather it involves an assessment and integration of those interests on the basis of a balanced hierarchy of values; ultimately, it demands a correct understanding of the dignity and rights of the person."

46. For a better understanding of the principle of subsidiarity, cf. Pius XI, *On Reconstructing the Social Order (Quadragesimo Anno)* (1931), no. 79, in *Contemporary Catholic Social Teaching* (Washington, D.C.: United States Catholic Conference, 1991), which states the following: "Just as it is gravely wrong to take from individuals what they can accomplish by their own initiative and industry and give it to the community, so also it is an injustice and at the same time a grave evil and disturbance of right order to assign to a greater and higher association what lesser and subordinate organizations can do. For every social activity ought of its very nature to furnish help [*subsidium*] to the members of the body social, and never destroy and absorb them."

47. *Economic Justice for All*, no. 196.

48. CCC, no. 2434.

49. John XXIII, *Peace on Earth (Pacem in Terris)* (Washington, D.C.: United States Catholic Conference, 1963), nos. 60-62.

50. *Economic Justice for All*, no. 123.

51. Ibid., no. 210.

52. GS, no. 75.

53. Cf. Administrative Board of the United States Catholic Conference, *A Commitment to All Generations: Social Security and the Common Good* (Washington, D.C.: United States Catholic Conference, 1999).

54. *Economic Justice for All*, no. 314.

55. Paul VI, *On Evangelization in the Modern World (Evangelii Nuntiandi)* (Washington, D.C.: United States Catholic Conference, 1975), no. 14.

56. Paul VI, Address for the Opening of the Third General Assembly of the Synod of Bishops (September 27, 1974), in *Acta Apostolicae Sedis* 66 (1974): 562.

57. CA, no. 57.

58. John Paul II, Address at Yankee Stadium, 350.

59. *Everyday Christianity*, 1.

60. CA, no. 57.

61. Ibid.

62. National Conference of Catholic Bishops, *Stewardship: A Disciple's Response* (Washington, D.C.: United States Catholic Conference, 1992).

63. GS, no. 19.

64. John Paul II, Address to the Representatives of Catholic Charities USA.